第二部分：**是非題**。共 6 題。請先看下面這張圖。每題你將會聽到 1 個短句。請仔細聽，聽到的句子和圖片的內容是不是相同呢？如果相同，請在答案紙上將 Ⓨ 塗黑；如果不同，請將 Ⓝ 塗黑。首先，請聽例題。

第 6-11 題

L

第三部分：**配合題**。共 7 題。每題你將會聽到 1 段敘述，請仔細聽，每題描述的是哪張圖片呢？請在答案紙上塗黑適合的選項。注意：你只會用到 7 張圖片。首先，請聽例題。

第 12-18 題

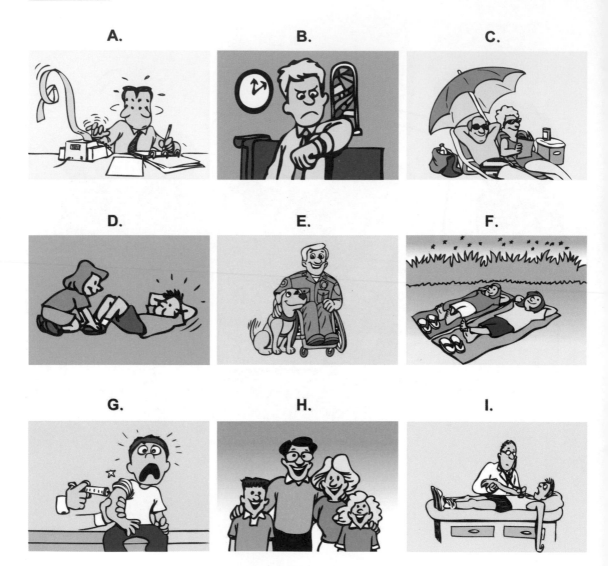

A.

B.

C.

D.

E.

F.

G.

H.

I.

第四部分：選擇題。共 7 題。請先看下面這張圖。每題你將會聽到 1 段對話，每段對話開始前，你會先聽到看和看到一個問題。請仔細聽問題和對話，並選一個最適合的答案，在答案紙上塗黑作答。首先，請聽例題。

例題： Where are the speakers?

    A. At school.

    B. At a bus stop.

    C. At a gym.

19. What does Helen ask for?

    A. Money for bus fare.

    B. A ride to school.

    C. Help with her homework.

20. How much did the man spend on apples?

    A. Twenty cents.

    B. One dollar.

    C. Two dollars.

21. Why isn't Dave going on the field trip?

    A. He forgot to have his parents sign a form.

    B. He refused to pay the fee.

    C. He doesn't feel well this morning.

L

22. Who went rock climbing with Mary?
    A. Her brother.
    B. Her sister.
    C. Her father.

23. When will Kevin and Ellen most likely visit Sogo?
    A. Early in the morning.
    B. During lunchtime.
    C. After dinner.

24. Why was Gloria late this morning?
    A. She missed her train.
    B. Her parents forgot to wake her.
    C. She slept through her alarm.

25. How often does Jerry use Youbike?
    A. Never.
    B. Sometimes.
    C. Often.

-☺☺聽力結束☺☺-

閱讀與寫作

共有 5 個部分，一共 40 題，作答時間 25 分鐘。

第一部分：**是非題**。共 20 題。請仔細閱讀，看看句子與圖片的內容是不是一樣呢？如果相同，請在答案紙上將 Ⓨ 塗黑；如果不同，請將 Ⓝ 塗黑。首先，請看例題。

例題：

例 1：This is a pair of sneakers.

例 2：They are blue and white.

兩題的正確答案都是 Ⓨ，你答對了嗎？現在我們開始第 1 題。

――――――――――――――――――――――――――――――

第 1-2 題

1.　This is a tea kettle.

2.　It is gray.

第 3-4 題

3.　The boy is smiling.

4.　He has a sore throat.

R

第 5-6 题

5. This is fast food.

6. They are finished eating.

第 7-8 题

7. They are seated at a table.

8. They are watching a film.

第 9-10 题

9. It is noon.

10. It is raining.

第 11-12 题

11. This is a mug of beer.

12. The glass is empty.

第 13-16 題

13. People come here to swim.
14. They are seated on a blue blanket.
15. They are seated in a circle.
16. There are trees behind the group.

第 17-20 題

17. The cat is sitting on the floor.
18. The girl on the right is reading a book.
19. The girl on the left is wearing red pajamas.
20. The woman in white is sewing.

R

第二部分：短文填空。這篇短文有 5 個空格，每個空格請從 A、B、C 選項選出一個最適合的答案，然後在答案紙上塗黑作答。首先，請看例題。

Keeping pets can teach you how to take ___(例題)___ of animals. If you have a dog, you will need to ___(21)___ it every day and give it food on time. You will also have to wash its body at least ___(22)___. But cats can clean themselves. So, some people think that keeping cats is much ___(23)___ keeping dogs. But other people think that dogs are nice to people. When we talk to them, dogs look at us as if they ___(24)___ understand what we say. In fact, many people think that their dog is their best friend. That is ___(25)___ more people want a dog at home than a cat.

例題： A. care（正確答案）   B. love   C. save

21.   A. walk   B. ride   C. dance
22.   A. one a month   B. two time a month   C. once a month
23.   A. as easy as   B. more easy than   C. easier than
24.   A. able to   B. are able to   C. can be able to
25.   A. why   B. how   C. what

第三部分：**閱讀理解**。共有兩篇短文。閱讀後，每題請根據文章內容選出一個最適合的答案，在答案紙上塗黑作答。

第 26-27 題

Sun. May 12th, 2016

Dear Diary,

Today is Mother's Day, but **it's not my day**...

In the early morning, I rode my bike to the flower

shop for a beautiful red carnation. The carnations

there were 1,000 for three, but I had only 100 dollars.

That was too expensive for me to buy one, so I left.

Then, on my way home, I fell down from the bike. My

T-shirt and pants became very dirty. But it was not the end. Just when

I got home, Mom was really angry to see my foolish look and shouted,

"Wash the clothes yourself." What an unlucky day!

Sad Helen

> 📖 rode 騎(過去式)　　　left 離開(過去式)
> fell off 跌落　　　pants 褲子
> clothes 衣服
> unlucky 不幸的

26. How did Helen go to the flower shop?

　　A. By bicycle.　　　B. By train.　　　C. By taxi.

27. Why was the mother angry?

　　A. Helen was late.

　　B. Helen didn't buy a carnation.

　　C. Helen looked dirty.

R

Super Cherry Sundae

To make a cherry sundae, you need a spoon of cherry jam, a half cup of cookies, a cup of cherry-flavored ice cream, and two fresh cherries.

=== HOW TO DO IT ===

FIRST, WASH CHERRIES.
SECOND, PUT THE CHERRY JAM IN A GLASS.
THIRD, PUT THE COOKIES ON TOP OF THE JAM.
NEXT, PUT INTO THE ICE CREAM.
LAST, PUT THE FRESH CHERRIES ON THE TOP.

📖 spoon 湯匙　　cherry 櫻桃
jam 果醬　　half 一半
flavored …口味的
top 頂端

28. In which book can we see this page?

    A. A picture book.   B. A comic book.

    C. A cookbook.

29. Jessica wants to make a cherry sundae for her family.

    Which doesn't she need?

    A. Ice cream.   B. Chocolate jam.

    C. Cookies.

30. Leo reads this page and makes a cherry sundae. What does his cherry sundae look like?

    A.

    B.

    C.

W

第四部分：**填填看和短句問答**。這是出現在旅遊時，的問題與回答。Ted 向巴士的導遊 Ms. Green 表達了他的感受，得到了她的回應。請依照圖片和文章的內容完成這對答的內容。<u>注意：答案請寫在答案紙上，第 31-33 題每個空格只需要填一個完整單字。</u>

Question

Hi Ms. Green, my (例題) **name** is Ted.

All of us are really enjoying this tour. You've (31) **s_____n** us so many interesting places. We've all learned a lot. However, we're (32) **l_____g** for something fun to do. Is there somewhere we can go to relax?

Answer

Hi Ted, I'm glad you asked.

Our next (33) **s_____p** will be Maple Lake. There we will have a picnic. Many people love to visit Maple Lake for the beautiful scenery and peaceful setting. We'll be there soon.

接下來，請根據上面兩封信的內容回答下面的問題。第 34-36 題請用句子回答。

例題：What has Ted seen? <u>He has seen interesting places.</u>

34. Where is Ted now? _____

35. What will they do at Maple Lake? _____

36. Who is Ms. Green? _____

第五部分：重組句子。共四題，請將每題的字詞重組成一個完整且有意義的句子。注意：答案請寫在答案紙上。題目裡的每一個字詞都要用到，增加或減少都會扣分。寫完後記得檢查大小寫和標點符號。首先，請看例題。

例題：There / beautiful / some / flowers. / are

正確答案是： <u>There are some beautiful flowers.</u>

寫完後，請記得檢查大小寫和標點符號。現在我們開始第 37 題。

37. outside? / cold / very / Is it

_____

38. tea. / cup of / I will / have a

_____

39. a letter. / A friend / me / wrote

_____

40. eat / here? / often / Do you

_____

-☺☺閱讀與寫作結束☺☺-

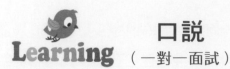

口説
（一對一面試）

第一部分：暖身、問候	（約 1 分鐘）
老師向學生打招呼	Good morning/afternoon. How are you today? May I have your score sheet? Your number is (准考證號碼).
老師自我介紹	My name is (老師名字). What's your name? How old are you?

第二部分(A)：朗讀句子	（約 1 分鐘）
老師拿出第二部分的圖片和描述圖片的三個句子請考生看	Now, (考生名字), please look at these sentences and this picture. These sentences describe the picture below. They are about a school cafeteria.
老師確認考生瞭解後，再繼續進行	Do you understand?
老師暫停 10 到 15 秒，讓考生閱讀句子	First, *just look at* the sentences.
老師指示考生開始朗讀句子	Now, *read* the sentences *aloud*.

第二部分(B)：描述圖片	（約 1 分鐘）
老師再一次指向第二部分的圖片	Now, (考生名字), look at the picture again, and answer my questions.
老師指向圖中間穿格子襯衫的男孩	What is the boy in the checkered shirt doing?
老師指向圖左下方穿黃色毛衣的女孩	What is the girl in the yellow sweater doing?
老師指向圖左下方正在哭泣的女孩	Who is crying?

1. This is a school cafeteria.

2. Some students are having lunch.

3. A girl is throwing something in the trash can.

第三部分：看圖説話	（約 2 分鐘）
老師給考生看第三部分的四張連環圖	In this part, you are going to tell a story based on these pictures.
老師説明連環圖的主題	These pictures show three people at an ice cream shop.
老師暫停約 10 秒，讓考生看圖	First, *look at* the four pictures.
待考生準備好，老師再繼續進行	Are you ready?
老師分別指向第 2、3、4 張圖	I will talk about picture 1. Then, you talk about pictures 2, 3, and 4.
老師指向第 1 張圖	Jeff offers to take Jane and Jenny for ice cream.
老師分別指向第 2、3、4 張圖，提示考生開始	Now, please talk about pictures 2, 3, and 4.

第四部分：回答問題	（約 1-2 分鐘）
老師收回第三部分的連環圖	Now, (考生名字), let's talk about you.
老師問考生右列問題	Do you like ice cream?
	How often do you eat ice cream?
	What about other snacks?
測驗結束	Thank you. This is the end of the test. Goodbye.

1

2

3

4

聽力、閱讀答案紙

Learning

准考證號碼：

○ 缺考紀錄(考生請勿自行劃記)

請沿虛線剪下

聽　力

1 Ⓨ Ⓝ	6 Ⓨ Ⓝ	12 Ⓐ Ⓑ Ⓒ Ⓓ Ⓔ Ⓕ Ⓖ Ⓗ Ⓘ	19 Ⓐ Ⓑ Ⓒ
2 Ⓨ Ⓝ	7 Ⓨ Ⓝ	13 Ⓐ Ⓑ Ⓒ Ⓓ Ⓔ Ⓕ Ⓖ Ⓗ Ⓘ	20 Ⓐ Ⓑ Ⓒ
2 Ⓨ Ⓝ	8 Ⓨ Ⓝ	14 Ⓐ Ⓑ Ⓒ Ⓓ Ⓔ Ⓕ Ⓖ Ⓗ Ⓘ	21 Ⓐ Ⓑ Ⓒ
4 Ⓨ Ⓝ	9 Ⓨ Ⓝ	15 Ⓐ Ⓑ Ⓒ Ⓓ Ⓔ Ⓕ Ⓖ Ⓗ Ⓘ	22 Ⓐ Ⓑ Ⓒ
5 Ⓨ Ⓝ	10 Ⓨ Ⓝ	16 Ⓐ Ⓑ Ⓒ Ⓓ Ⓔ Ⓕ Ⓖ Ⓗ Ⓘ	23 Ⓐ Ⓑ Ⓒ
	11 Ⓨ Ⓝ	17 Ⓐ Ⓑ Ⓒ Ⓓ Ⓔ Ⓕ Ⓖ Ⓗ Ⓘ	24 Ⓐ Ⓑ Ⓒ
		18 Ⓐ Ⓑ Ⓒ Ⓓ Ⓔ Ⓕ Ⓖ Ⓗ Ⓘ	25 Ⓐ Ⓑ Ⓒ

閱　讀

1 Ⓨ Ⓝ	11 Ⓨ Ⓝ	21 Ⓐ Ⓑ Ⓒ
2 Ⓨ Ⓝ	12 Ⓨ Ⓝ	22 Ⓐ Ⓑ Ⓒ
2 Ⓨ Ⓝ	13 Ⓨ Ⓝ	23 Ⓐ Ⓑ Ⓒ
4 Ⓨ Ⓝ	14 Ⓨ Ⓝ	24 Ⓐ Ⓑ Ⓒ
5 Ⓨ Ⓝ	15 Ⓨ Ⓝ	25 Ⓐ Ⓑ Ⓒ
6 Ⓨ Ⓝ	16 Ⓨ Ⓝ	26 Ⓐ Ⓑ Ⓒ
7 Ⓨ Ⓝ	17 Ⓨ Ⓝ	27 Ⓐ Ⓑ Ⓒ
8 Ⓨ Ⓝ	18 Ⓨ Ⓝ	28 Ⓐ Ⓑ Ⓒ
9 Ⓨ Ⓝ	19 Ⓨ Ⓝ	29 Ⓐ Ⓑ Ⓒ
10 Ⓨ Ⓝ	20 Ⓨ Ⓝ	30 Ⓐ Ⓑ Ⓒ

注意事項

1. 限用2B鉛筆作答。
2. 劃記要粗黑、清晰、不可出格，擦拭要清潔。

作答樣例：

正確方式　●

錯誤方式　✓ ✗ •

學習出版有限公司

03797706-30

准考證號碼：

例答	name
31.	
32.	
33.	

例答	He has seen interesting places.
34.	
35.	
36.	

例答	There are some beautiful flowers.
37.	
38.	
39.	
40.	

L

TEST 2

聽力：共有 4 個部分，一共 25 題。每題播放 2 次。

第一部分：是非題。共 5 題。每題你將會聽到 1 個短句。請仔細聽，聽到的句子和圖片是不是相同呢？如果相同，請在答案紙上將 Ⓨ 塗黑；如果不同，請將 Ⓝ 塗黑。首先，請聽例題。

例題：

3.

1.

4.

2.

5.

第二部分：**是非題**。共 6 題。請先看下面這張圖。每題你將會聽到 1 個短句。請仔細聽，聽到的句子和圖片的內容是不是相同呢？如果相同，請在答案紙上將 Ⓨ 塗黑；如果不同，請將 Ⓝ 塗黑。首先，請聽例題。

第 6-11 題

L

第三部分：**配合題**。共 7 題。每題你將會聽到 1 段敘述，請仔細聽，每題描述的是哪張圖片呢？請在答案紙上塗黑適合的選項。注意：你只會用到 7 張圖片。首先，請聽例題。

<u>第 12-18 題</u>

A. **B.** **C.**

D. **E.** **F.**

G. **H.** **I.**

第四部分：選擇題。共 7 題。請先看下面這張圖。每題你將會聽到 1 段對話，每段對話開始前，你會先聽到看和看到一個問題。請仔細聽問題和對話，並選一個最適合的答案，在答案紙上塗黑作答。首先，請聽例題。

例題： Where are the speakers?

    A. At school.

    B. At a bus stop.

    C. At a gym.

19. Why can't Jack go swimming?

    A. He has a cold.

    B. He doesn't know how.

    C. He is afraid of water.

20. What did Marcy do?

    A. She went on vacation.

    B. She got a haircut.

    C. She put on some weight.

21. Where is Frank going?

    A. To school.

    B. To the park.

    C. To Joe's house.

L

22. Where is Peter's science textbook?
    A. In the kitchen.
    B. In his bedroom.
    C. In his backpack.

23. Which class will they have next?
    A. History.
    B. PE.
    C. Chinese.

24. Who will take Cindy to see the movie?
    A. Her dad.
    B. Her mom.
    C. Steve.

25. Why is Mike still in bed?
    A. There's no school today.
    B. He didn't hear his alarm.
    C. He doesn't feel well.

-☺☺聽力結束☺☺-

閱讀與寫作

共有 5 個部分，一共 40 題，作答時間 25 分鐘。

第一部分：是非題。共 20 題。請仔細閱讀，看看句子與圖片的內容是不是一樣呢？如果相同，請在答案紙上將 Ⓨ 塗黑；如果不同，請將 Ⓝ 塗黑。首先，請看例題。

例題：

例 1：This is a pair of sneakers.

例 2：They are blue and white.

兩題的正確答案都是 Ⓨ，你答對了嗎？現在我們開始第 1 題。

───────────────────────────────

第 1-2 題

1.　He is sitting on a chair.

2.　He is standing near a window.

第 3-4 題

3.　They are at an airport.

4.　They are on an airplane.

R

第 5-6 題

5. One girl has green hair.

6. One girl has blond hair.

第 7-8 題

7. They are holding hands.

8. They are studying.

第 9-10 題

9. The girls are wearing skirts.

10. The boys are wearing hats.

第 11-12 題

11. Laura loves fast food.

12. Laura is exercising.

第 13-16 題

13. They are indoors.
14. The girl is behind the tree.
15. One boy is holding a net.
16. They are fishing.

第 17-20 題

17. They are at the beach.
18. They are playing a game.
19. One boy is digging in the sand.
20. The girl is leaning against the surfboard.

R

第二部分：短文填空。這篇短文有 5 個空格，每個空格請從 A、B、C 選項選出一個最適合的答案，然後在答案紙上塗黑作答。首先，請看例題。

(In a bookstore.)

Shelly: Excuse me. Do you ___(例題)___ dictionaries?

 Clerk: Of course.

Shelly: ___(21)___ are they?

 Clerk: Please come with me.

(In front of the dictionaries.)

 Clerk: What kind of dictionary do you need?

Shelly: A picture English dictionary ___(22)___ my little sister. She is
　　　　learning English in her school.

 Clerk: Here! We have five different picture dictionaries. You can take a
　　　　look.

Shelly: ___(23)___ is the most popular?

 Clerk: Both *Wonder Word Book* and *Smart Picture Dictionary* sell very
　　　　well *Wonder Word Book* is mainly for kids, so it doesn't have too
　　　　___(24)___ words.

Shelly: Okay, I will take *Smart Picture Dictionary*. I may use it ___(25)___.

 Clerk: Good choice!

> 📖 excuse me 請問
> dictionary 字典
> kind 種類
> mainly 主要地

例題：A. show　　　　B. have（正確答案）　　　　C. keep

21.　A. What　　　　B. Who　　　　　C. Where
22.　A. for　　　　　B. at　　　　　　C. to
23.　A. Who　　　　B. What　　　　　C. Which
24.　A. any　　　　　B. many　　　　　C. much
25.　A. always　　　B. sometimes　　C. usually

第三部分：**閱讀理解**。共有兩篇短文。閱讀後，每題請根據文章內容選出一個最適合的答案，在答案紙上塗黑作答。

第 26-27 題

From	Huck@hotmail.com
To	Tom@yahoo.com
Subject	The Reunion

Dear Tom,

    How are you doing? I miss you very much. We have a reunion party at Amanda's Café at 2:00 p.m. this Sunday. Many old friends will come. By the way, Miss Chen, our favorite English teacher, will come, too. Can you come to join us? Please let me know you will come or not. Remember to call me before Wednesday. My telephone number is 2201-1234.

Your friend,
Huck Wang

26. When is the reunion party?
    A. On Wednesday afternoon.
    B. On Sunday evening.
    C. On Sunday afternoon.

27. Which one is true?
    A. Huck and Amanda are classmates.
    B. Amanda is Tom's student.
    C. Miss Chen is Tom and Huck's teacher.

R

Here is an ad from Mama's Supermarket. Read the ad and answer the following questions.

📖 ad 廣告　　grape 葡萄　　save 節省

28. How much is a can of chicken soup at Mama's Supermarket?
    A. NT$29.   B. NT$49.
    C. NT$229.

29. Jenny needs three bottles of apple juice. How much are they at
    Mama's Supermarket?
    A. NT$49.   B. NT$58.
    C. NT$98.

30. Bill buys two boxes of black tea from Mama's Supermarket. How
    much can he save?
    A. NT$70.   B. NT$140.
    C. NT$658.

W

第四部分：填填看和短句問答。這是學生和老師問題與答覆的兩封信。Wendy 寫信給老師 Mr. Gordon，得到了她的回信和建議。請依照圖片和文章的內容完成這兩封信。注意：答案請寫在答案紙上，第 31-33 題每個空格只需要填一個完整單字。

Question

Dear Mr. Gordon,

I'm very（例題）**worried** about the exam. I (31) **s_____d** until two o'clock in the morning last night. I really tried my best and I hope I did well. Can you tell me my grade?

Sincerely,

Wendy

Answer

Dear Wendy,

(32) **R_____x**! You did fine on the test. Actually, you did better than fine. You got a (33) **p_____t** score. I'm very proud of you for studying so hard. As you can see, it paid off for you!

Regards,

Mr. Gordon

接下來，請根據上面兩封信的內容回答下面的問題。第 34-36 題請用句子回答。

例題：What is Mr. Gordon?　**He is a teacher.**

34.　How does Wendy feel?　　　　＿＿＿＿＿＿＿＿＿＿＿＿＿

35.　What did Wendy do last night?　＿＿＿＿＿＿＿＿＿＿＿＿＿

36.　How did Wendy do on the exam?　＿＿＿＿＿＿＿＿＿＿＿＿＿

第五部分：重組句子。共四題，請將每題的字詞重組成一個完整且有意義的句子。注意：答案請寫在答案紙上。題目裡的每一個字詞都要用到，增加或減少都會扣分。寫完後記得檢查大小寫和標點符號。首先，請看例題。

例題：There / beautiful / some / flowers. / are

正確答案是：　**There are some beautiful flowers.**

寫完後，請記得檢查大小寫和標點符號。現在我們開始第 37 題。

37.　abroad? / Have you / ever / traveled

＿＿＿＿＿＿＿＿＿＿＿＿＿＿＿＿＿＿＿＿＿＿＿

38.　that? / eat / Are you / going to

＿＿＿＿＿＿＿＿＿＿＿＿＿＿＿＿＿＿＿＿＿＿＿

39.　kitchen. / dancing / Dave / is / in the

＿＿＿＿＿＿＿＿＿＿＿＿＿＿＿＿＿＿＿＿＿＿＿

40.　exciting. / The / movie / was

＿＿＿＿＿＿＿＿＿＿＿＿＿＿＿＿＿＿＿＿＿＿＿

-☺☺閱讀與寫作結束☺☺-

口説 （一對一面試）

第一部分：暖身、問候	（約 1 分鐘）

老師向學生打招呼

Good morning/afternoon. How are you today?

May I have your score sheet?
Your number is (准考證號碼).

老師自我介紹

My name is (老師名字). What's your name?

How old are you?

第二部分(A)：朗讀句子	（約 1 分鐘）

老師拿出第二部分的圖片和描述圖片的三個句子請考生看

Now, (考生名字), please look at these sentences and this picture. These sentences describe the picture below. They are about a swimming pool.

老師確認考生瞭解後，再繼續進行

Do you understand?

老師暫停 10 到 15 秒，讓考生閱讀句子

First, *just look at* the sentences.

老師指示考生開始朗讀句子

Now, *read* the sentences *aloud*.

第二部分(B)：描述圖片	（約 1 分鐘）

老師再一次指向第二部分的圖片

Now, (考生名字), look at the picture again, and answer my questions.

老師指向游泳池旁邊的球或是游泳圈

What can you find beside the swimming pool?

老師指向圖右上方穿灰色泳裝的男孩

What is the boy in the gray swimsuit doing?

老師指向穿粉紅色泳裝的女孩

What is the girl in the pink swimsuit doing?

1. This is a public swimming pool.

2. Some people are swimming in the pool.

3. Jason is wearing a blue swim suit.

第三部分：看圖說話	**（約 2 分鐘）**
老師給考生看第三部分的四張連環圖	In this part, you are going to tell a story based on these pictures.
老師說明連環圖的主題	These pictures show a mother and two children, Tina and John.
老師暫停約 10 秒，讓考生看圖	First, *look at* the four pictures.
待考生準備好，老師再繼續進行	Are you ready?
老師分別指向第 2、3、4 張圖	I will talk about picture 1. Then, you talk about pictures 2, 3, and 4.
老師指向第 1 張圖	Mom went to work this morning.
老師分別指向第 2、3、4 張圖，提示考生開始	Now, please talk about pictures 2, 3, and 4.

第四部分：回答問題	**（約 1-2 分鐘）**
老師收回第三部分的連環圖	Now, (考生名字), let's talk about you.
老師問考生右列問題	How many people are there in your family?
	How often does your family eat out?
	What do you and your family like to do together?
測驗結束	Thank you. This is the end of the test. Goodbye.

聽力、閱讀答案紙

准考證號碼：

SAMPLE

■ ○ 缺考紀錄(考生請勿自行劃記)

聽　力

1 Ⓨ Ⓝ	6 Ⓨ Ⓝ	12 Ⓐ Ⓑ Ⓒ Ⓓ Ⓔ Ⓕ Ⓖ Ⓗ Ⓘ	19 Ⓐ Ⓑ Ⓒ
2 Ⓨ Ⓝ	7 Ⓨ Ⓝ	13 Ⓐ Ⓑ Ⓒ Ⓓ Ⓔ Ⓕ Ⓖ Ⓗ Ⓘ	20 Ⓐ Ⓑ Ⓒ
2 Ⓨ Ⓝ	8 Ⓨ Ⓝ	14 Ⓐ Ⓑ Ⓒ Ⓓ Ⓔ Ⓕ Ⓖ Ⓗ Ⓘ	21 Ⓐ Ⓑ Ⓒ
4 Ⓨ Ⓝ	9 Ⓨ Ⓝ	15 Ⓐ Ⓑ Ⓒ Ⓓ Ⓔ Ⓕ Ⓖ Ⓗ Ⓘ	22 Ⓐ Ⓑ Ⓒ
5 Ⓨ Ⓝ	10 Ⓨ Ⓝ	16 Ⓐ Ⓑ Ⓒ Ⓓ Ⓔ Ⓕ Ⓖ Ⓗ Ⓘ	23 Ⓐ Ⓑ Ⓒ
	11 Ⓨ Ⓝ	17 Ⓐ Ⓑ Ⓒ Ⓓ Ⓔ Ⓕ Ⓖ Ⓗ Ⓘ	24 Ⓐ Ⓑ Ⓒ
		18 Ⓐ Ⓑ Ⓒ Ⓓ Ⓔ Ⓕ Ⓖ Ⓗ Ⓘ	25 Ⓐ Ⓑ Ⓒ

閱　讀

1 Ⓨ Ⓝ	11 Ⓨ Ⓝ	21 Ⓐ Ⓑ Ⓒ
2 Ⓨ Ⓝ	12 Ⓨ Ⓝ	22 Ⓐ Ⓑ Ⓒ
2 Ⓨ Ⓝ	13 Ⓨ Ⓝ	23 Ⓐ Ⓑ Ⓒ
4 Ⓨ Ⓝ	14 Ⓨ Ⓝ	24 Ⓐ Ⓑ Ⓒ
5 Ⓨ Ⓝ	15 Ⓨ Ⓝ	25 Ⓐ Ⓑ Ⓒ
6 Ⓨ Ⓝ	16 Ⓨ Ⓝ	26 Ⓐ Ⓑ Ⓒ
7 Ⓨ Ⓝ	17 Ⓨ Ⓝ	27 Ⓐ Ⓑ Ⓒ
8 Ⓨ Ⓝ	18 Ⓨ Ⓝ	28 Ⓐ Ⓑ Ⓒ
9 Ⓨ Ⓝ	19 Ⓨ Ⓝ	29 Ⓐ Ⓑ Ⓒ
10 Ⓨ Ⓝ	20 Ⓨ Ⓝ	30 Ⓐ Ⓑ Ⓒ

注意事項

1. 限用2B鉛筆作答。
2. 劃記要粗黑、清晰、不可出格，擦拭要清潔。

作答樣例：

　正確方式 ●

　錯誤方式 ☑ ⊗ ●

請沿虛線剪下

學習出版有限公司

03797706-30

准考證號碼：

例答	worried

31.	

32.	

33.	

例答	He is a teacher.

34.	

35.	

36.	

例答	There are some beautiful flowers.

37.	

38.	

39.	

40.	

學習出版有限公司

L

TEST 3

聽力：共有 4 個部分，一共 25 題。每題播放 2 次。

第一部分：是非題。共 5 題。每題你將會聽到 1 個短句。請仔細聽，聽到的句子和圖片是不是相同呢？如果相同，請在答案紙上將 Ⓨ 塗黑；如果不同，請將 Ⓝ 塗黑。首先，請聽例題。

例題：

3.

1.

4.

2.

5.

第二部分：是非題。共 6 題。請先看下面這張圖。每題你將會聽到 1 個短句。請仔細聽，聽到的句子和圖片的內容是不是相同呢？如果相同，請在答案紙上將 Ⓨ 塗黑；如果不同，請將 Ⓝ 塗黑。首先，請聽例題。

<u>第 6-11 題</u>

L

第三部分：**配合題**。共 7 題。每題你將會聽到 1 段敘述，請仔細聽，每題描述的是哪張圖片呢？請在答案紙上塗黑適合的選項。注意：你只會用到 7 張圖片。首先，請聽例題。

<u>第 12-18 題</u>

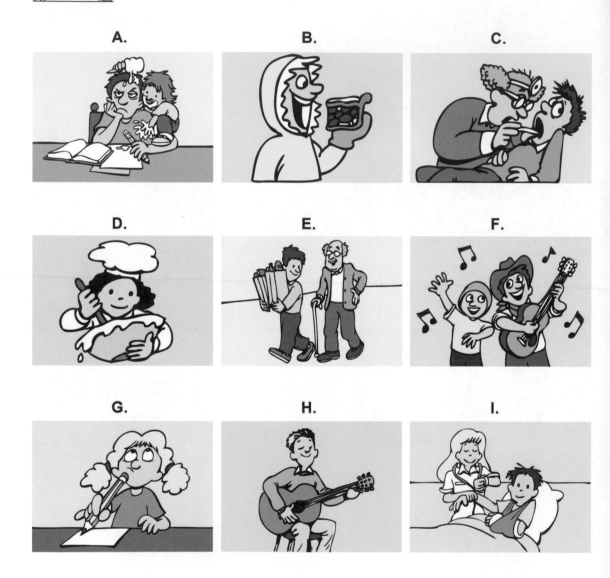

第四部分：選擇題。共 7 題。請先看下面這張圖。每題你將會聽到 1 段對話，每段對話開始前，你會先聽到看和看到一個問題。請仔細聽問題和對話，並選一個最適合的答案，在答案紙上塗黑作答。首先，請聽例題。

例題： Where are the speakers?

    A. At school.

    B. At a bus stop.

    C. At a gym.

19. What is the woman going to do?

    A. Make dinner.

    B. Take a nap.

    C. Make a phone call.

20. Where did the man see Kenneth?

    A. At the gym.

    B. At school.

    C. At work.

21. What do we know about Tommy?

    A. He is older than Lucy.

    B. He is younger than Lucy.

    C. He is Lucy's classmate.

L

22. What does Brian want to do?
    A. See Ms. Wang after class.
    B. Skip band practice.
    C. Ask Ms. Wang a question.

23. What was Frankie supposed to do for Nick?
    A. Take him to the dentist.
    B. Tell Lucy that he wouldn't meet her in the cafeteria.
    C. Talk to Lucy about their science project.

24. When is the boy's graduation party?
    A. This weekend.
    B. Next weekend.
    C. On Monday.

25. What is the problem with Donald?
    A. He threw away math textbook.
    B. He left his textbook at home.
    C. He did not write his name on his math textbook.

-☺☺聽力結束☺☺-

閱讀與寫作

共有 5 個部分，一共 40 題，作答時間 25 分鐘。

第一部分：**是非題**。共 20 題。請仔細閱讀，看看句子與圖片的內容是不是一樣呢？如果相同，請在答案紙上將 ⓨ 塗黑；如果不同，請將 ⓝ 塗黑。首先，請看例題。

例題：

例 1：This is a pair of sneakers.

例 2：They are blue and white.

兩題的正確答案都是 ⓨ，你答對了嗎？現在我們開始第 1 題。

第 1-2 題

1. She is sitting at a desk.

2. She is typing a letter.

第 3-4 題

3. The teacher is telling a story.

4. Four children are seated on the floor.

R

第 5-6 題

5. Matt has lost his wallet.

6. Matt is wearing a striped shirt.

第 7-8 題

7. The boys are hugging.

8. The boys are laughing.

第 9-10 題

9. Brendan is walking his dog.

10. The dog is on a leash.

第 11-12 題

11. Tim is wearing a white sweater.

12. His mom is wearing a blue skirt.

第 13-16 題

13. They are farmers.
14. They are watching television.
15. They are planting seeds.
16. They are outdoors.

第 17-20 題

17. The boy is in bed.
18. The man is reading a book.
19. There is a clock on the wall.
20. There is a lamp on the nightstand.

R

A loud noise from next door woke me up. I looked at my ___(例題)___ .
It was 7 o'clock. "What's the noise? Are Mr. and Mrs. Jones having a
___(21)___ again?" I thought. "But that doesn't sound like Mr. Jones. Who's
that man?" About half an hour later, I heard Mrs. Jones ___(22)___ for help.
I put on my clothes and ran to their house. I didn't knock on the door. I
just stood at the door. I could tell that the man was angry because he
shouted many times! I heard him say, "Tell Kevin he will be in trouble if
he ___(23)___ my money back tomorrow before 10 o'clock." I was scared
then. "What if the man has ___(24)___ ? Should I just call the police?" I
thought. When I ___(25)___ about what to do, my cell phone rang...

例題： A. wall   B. bed   C. watch（正確答案）

21.   A. fight   B. meeting   C. barbecue

22.   A. to cry   B. was crying   C. crying

23.   A. doesn't give   B. won't give   C. didn't give

24.   A. some butter   B. a fork   C. a knife

25.   A. think   B. was thinking   C. thought

第三部分：閱讀理解。共有兩篇短文。閱讀後，每題請根據文章內容選出一個最適合的答案，在答案紙上塗黑作答。

第 26-27 題

>   Lots of people make friends on the Internet. Amy does, too. But she is careful about that. She uses a different name on the Internet. She doesn't tell her Internet friends about her home. She doesn't give them her home phone number, either. She gives a few Internet friends her cellphone number. Some people on the Internet are not nice. Amy knows that, too. She doesn't talk to those people at all.
>
>   Amy gets together with a few Internet friends. She meets them at restaurants and coffee shops. Those places are OK. There are lots of other people around.

> 📖 careful 小心的   a few 一些

26. What does Amy change（改變）on the Internet?
    A. Her number.
    B. Her home.
    C. Her name.

27. What can a few of Amy's Internet friends do?
    A. They can call her.
    B. They can drive her home.
    C. They can visit her home.

R

Four students of Class 601 want to take art class next year. They took several tests last week. Here are their grades.

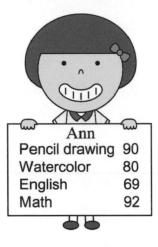

Ann	
Pencil drawing	90
Watercolor	80
English	69
Math	92

Ken	
Pencil drawing	95
Watercolor	95
English	85
Math	95

Bill	
Pencil drawing	80
Watercolor	70
English	92
Math	80

Meg	
Pencil drawing	85
Watercolor	90
English	100
Math	70

28. Those who want to go to the art class must get 70 or above in English and math, and get 80 or above in pencil drawing and watercolor. How many students aren't able to go to the art class?

    A. Zero.

    B. One.

    C. Two.

29. Which is NOT true about the four students' written tests?

    A. Meg's English is the best.

    B. Ken's math is the worst.

    C. Meg needs to do more math exercises.

30. Here is what the teacher wrote to one of the students.

    You did great in drawing. Don't be sad about your English. You're almost there. I'm sure you'll do better next time.

    Who is that student?

    A. Ann.

    B. Ken.

    C. Bill.

W

第四部分：填填看和短句問答。這是出現在班上公佈欄的兩封信。Paul 寫信給班導師 Ms. Liu，想尋求舉辦活動的許可，得到了她的回信和建議。請依照圖片和文章的內容完成這兩封信。注意：答案請寫在答案紙上，第 31-33 題每個空格只需要填一個完整單字。

Question

Dear Ms. Liu,

(例題) **Christmas** is (31) c_____g. Many students have been studying hard all semester. Maybe we could use a break. I was wondering if we could have a party to celebrate the holiday?

Sincerely,
Paul

Answer

Dear Paul,

Of course we can have a Christmas party, Paul. I think that's a great idea! We can give each other (32) g_____s and I will bring something to eat and drink. We can also have a Christmas (33) t_____e. Would you be willing to help me decorate the classroom? Let me know.

Best,
Ms. Liu

接下來，請根據上面兩封信的內容回答下面的問題。第 34-36 題請用句子回答。

例題：Where will the party be? <u>**It will be in the classroom.**</u>

34. Who is Paul? _____

35. What holiday is coming? _____

36. What does Paul ask Ms. Liu? _____

第五部分：重組句子。 共四題，請將每題的字詞重組成一個完整且有意義的句子。注意：答案請寫在答案紙上。題目裡的每一個字詞都要用到，增加或減少都會扣分。寫完後記得檢查大小寫和標點符號。首先，請看例題。

例題：There / beautiful / some / flowers. / are

正確答案是： <u>**There are some beautiful flowers.**</u>

寫完後，請記得檢查大小寫和標點符號。現在我們開始第 37 題。

37. book / on the desk / open. / The / is

_____

38. hands. / The boy / looking / is / at / his

_____

39. before / to bed? / Do you / going / read / ever

_____

40. weigh? / How / much / you / do

_____

-☺☺閱讀與寫作結束☺☺-

 口説
（一對一面試）

第一部分：暖身、問候　　　　　　　（約 1 分鐘）

老師向學生打招呼	Good morning/afternoon.　How are you today?
	May I have your score sheet? Your number is (准考證號碼).
老師自我介紹	My name is (老師名字).　What's your name?
	How old are you?

第二部分(A)：朗讀句子　　　　　　　（約 1 分鐘）

老師拿出第二部分的圖片和描述圖片的三個句子請考生看	Now, (考生名字), please look at these sentences and this picture.　These sentences describe the picture below.　They are about a yard sale.
老師確認考生瞭解後，再繼續進行	Do you understand?
老師暫停 10 到 15 秒，讓考生閱讀句子	First, *just look at* the sentences.
老師指示考生開始朗讀句子	Now, *read* the sentences *aloud*.

第二部分(B)：描述圖片　　　　　　　（約 1 分鐘）

老師再一次指向第二部分的圖片	Now, (考生名字), look at the picture again, and answer my questions.
老師指向亨利販售的物品	Is Henry selling a baseball bat?
老師指向圖中女士的洋裝	What color is the woman's dress?
老師指向亨利的左手	Where is Henry's left hand?

1. Henry is having a yard sale.

2. He is selling the items he doesn't want or use anymore.

3. He has set up a table in the front yard of his house.

第三部分：看圖説話	（約 2 分鐘）

老師給考生看第三部分的四張連環圖	In this part, you are going to tell a story based on these pictures.
老師説明連環圖的主題	These pictures show what happened to John and Sam when they went hiking last Sunday.
老師暫停約 10 秒，讓考生看圖	First, *look at* the four pictures.
待考生準備好，老師再繼續進行	Are you ready?
老師分別指向第 2、3、4 張圖	I will talk about picture 1. Then, you talk about pictures 2, 3, and 4.
老師指向第 1 張圖	John and Sam went hiking in the woods to see if they could find a bear.
老師分別指向第 2、3、4 張圖，提示考生開始	Now, please talk about pictures 2, 3, and 4.

第四部分：回答問題	（約 1-2 分鐘）

老師收回第三部分的連環圖	Now, (考生名字), let's talk about you.
老師問考生右列問題	Have you ever seen a bear?
	Do you ever go hiking?
	What is your favorite outdoor activity?
測驗結束	Thank you. This is the end of the test. Goodbye.

1

2

3

4

聽力、閱讀答案紙

Learning

准考證號碼：

○ 缺考紀錄(考生請勿自行劃記)

聽　力

1 Ⓨ Ⓝ	6 Ⓨ Ⓝ	12 Ⓐ Ⓑ Ⓒ Ⓓ Ⓔ Ⓕ Ⓖ Ⓗ Ⓘ	19 Ⓐ Ⓑ Ⓒ
2 Ⓨ Ⓝ	7 Ⓨ Ⓝ	13 Ⓐ Ⓑ Ⓒ Ⓓ Ⓔ Ⓕ Ⓖ Ⓗ Ⓘ	20 Ⓐ Ⓑ Ⓒ
2 Ⓨ Ⓝ	8 Ⓨ Ⓝ	14 Ⓐ Ⓑ Ⓒ Ⓓ Ⓔ Ⓕ Ⓖ Ⓗ Ⓘ	21 Ⓐ Ⓑ Ⓒ
4 Ⓨ Ⓝ	9 Ⓨ Ⓝ	15 Ⓐ Ⓑ Ⓒ Ⓓ Ⓔ Ⓕ Ⓖ Ⓗ Ⓘ	22 Ⓐ Ⓑ Ⓒ
5 Ⓨ Ⓝ	10 Ⓨ Ⓝ	16 Ⓐ Ⓑ Ⓒ Ⓓ Ⓔ Ⓕ Ⓖ Ⓗ Ⓘ	23 Ⓐ Ⓑ Ⓒ
	11 Ⓨ Ⓝ	17 Ⓐ Ⓑ Ⓒ Ⓓ Ⓔ Ⓕ Ⓖ Ⓗ Ⓘ	24 Ⓐ Ⓑ Ⓒ
		18 Ⓐ Ⓑ Ⓒ Ⓓ Ⓔ Ⓕ Ⓖ Ⓗ Ⓘ	25 Ⓐ Ⓑ Ⓒ

閱　讀

1 Ⓨ Ⓝ	11 Ⓨ Ⓝ	21 Ⓐ Ⓑ Ⓒ
2 Ⓨ Ⓝ	12 Ⓨ Ⓝ	22 Ⓐ Ⓑ Ⓒ
2 Ⓨ Ⓝ	13 Ⓨ Ⓝ	23 Ⓐ Ⓑ Ⓒ
4 Ⓨ Ⓝ	14 Ⓨ Ⓝ	24 Ⓐ Ⓑ Ⓒ
5 Ⓨ Ⓝ	15 Ⓨ Ⓝ	25 Ⓐ Ⓑ Ⓒ
6 Ⓨ Ⓝ	16 Ⓨ Ⓝ	26 Ⓐ Ⓑ Ⓒ
7 Ⓨ Ⓝ	17 Ⓨ Ⓝ	27 Ⓐ Ⓑ Ⓒ
8 Ⓨ Ⓝ	18 Ⓨ Ⓝ	28 Ⓐ Ⓑ Ⓒ
9 Ⓨ Ⓝ	19 Ⓨ Ⓝ	29 Ⓐ Ⓑ Ⓒ
10 Ⓨ Ⓝ	20 Ⓨ Ⓝ	30 Ⓐ Ⓑ Ⓒ

注意事項

1. 限用2B鉛筆作答。
2. 劃記要粗黑、清晰、不可出格，擦拭要清潔。

作答樣例：
正確方式 ●
錯誤方式 ✓ ⊗ ●

學習出版有限公司

03797706-30

寫作答案紙

准考證號碼：

例答	Christmas
31.	
32.	
33.	
例答	It will be in the classroom.
34.	
35.	
36.	
例答	There are some beautiful flowers.
37.	
38.	
39.	
40.	

L

TEST 4

聽力：共有 4 個部分，一共 25 題。每題播放 2 次。

第一部分：**是非題。**共 5 題。每題你將會聽到 1 個短句。請仔細聽，聽到的句子和圖片是不是相同呢？如果相同，請在答案紙上將 Ⓨ 塗黑；如果不同，請將 Ⓝ 塗黑。首先，請聽例題。

例題：

3.

1.

4.

2.

5.

第二部分：是非題。共 6 題。請先看下面這張圖。每題你將會聽到 1 個短句。請仔細聽，聽到的句子和圖片的內容是不是相同呢？如果相同，請在答案紙上將 Ⓨ 塗黑；如果不同，請將 Ⓝ 塗黑。首先，請聽例題。

<u>第 6-11 題</u>

L

第三部分：**配合題**。共 7 題。每題你將會聽到 1 段敘述，請仔細聽，每題描述的是哪張圖片呢？請在答案紙上塗黑適合的選項。注意：你只會用到 7 張圖片。首先，請聽例題。

<u>第 12-18 題</u>

第四部分：選擇題。共 7 題。請先看下面這張圖。每題你將會聽到 1 段對話，每段對話開始前，你會先聽到看和看到一個問題。請仔細聽問題和對話，並選一個最適合的答案，在答案紙上塗黑作答。首先，請聽例題。

例題： Where are the speakers?

    A. At school.

    B. At a bus stop.

    C. At a gym.

19. Where does the girl want to go?

    A. To the library.

    B. To the post office.

    C. To the museum.

20. What did Luke invite Martha to do?

    A. Take piano lessons on Saturday afternoon.

    B. Go bowling on Saturday evening.

    C. Play basketball on Sunday morning.

21. What is one way Debbie could make the Earth a cleaner place?

    A. By walking to school.

    B. By studying at night.

    C. By staying home in the winter.

22. What will Ashley have for lunch?

    A. Whatever is being served in the cafeteria.

    B. Some carrot sticks.

    C. A ham sandwich.

23. What will Victoria do tomorrow morning?

    A. Go on a hike.

    B. Study for a test.

    C. Carry an umbrella.

24. Who went looking for the dog with Oscar?

    A. His teacher.

    B. His father.

    C. His brother.

25. Which tie will the man most likely wear?

    A. The blue tie.

    B. The brown tie.

    C. The green and yellow-striped tie.

-☺☺聽力結束☺☺-

閱讀與寫作

共有 5 個部分，一共 40 題，作答時間 25 分鐘。

第一部分：**是非題**。共 20 題。請仔細閱讀，看看句子與圖片的內容是不是一樣呢？如果相同，請在答案紙上將 Ⓨ 塗黑；如果不同，請將 Ⓝ 塗黑。首先，請看例題。

例題：

例 1：This is a pair of sneakers.

例 2：They are blue and white.

兩題的正確答案都是 Ⓨ，你答對了嗎？現在我們開始第 1 題。

第 1-2 題

1. A boy is sitting in a chair.

2. They are both standing.

第 3-4 題

3. The woman has short hair.

4. They are all wearing pants.

R

5. The girl is on the bus.

6. They are boarding a train.

7. The man has long hair.

8. The man is wearing a hat.

9. They are in a library.

10. The boy with blond hair is behind the counter.

11. There are four boys in the picture.

12. The door is open.

第 13-16 題

13. There is a bucket on the floor.
14. The girl is sitting on the floor.
15. There are pictures on the wall.
16. The girl is writing a letter.

第 17-20 題

17. There is a father, a mother, and two children in the picture.
18. The father has the boy on his shoulders.
19. The mother is carrying a purse.
20. The girl is riding a bicycle.

R

第二部分：**短文填空**。這篇短文有 5 個空格，每個空格請從 A、B、C 選項選出一個最適合的答案，然後在答案紙上塗黑作答。首先，請看例題。

Sunny: Look at the boy over there. He's so _____（例題）_____.

Kate: Yeah! He is Mark, a new student in my class.

Sunny: I __(21)__. Is he a Taiwanese?

Kate: No, he is from Japan. He is here only __(22)__ three weeks.

Sunny: Can he speak Chinese?

Kate: __(23)__. He is good at it.

Sunny: Cool! By the way, __(24)__ he play basketball?

Kate: Yes, he plays basketball after school every day. Look! He __(25)__ a basketball now.

Sunny: Maybe we can play with him. Let's go!

> 📖 by the way 順便一提

例題：A. heavy B. tall（正確答案） C. slow

21. A. watch B. see C. look

22. A. with B. on C. for

23. A. Sure. B. Too bad. C. What's up?

24. A. Can't B. Is C. Does

25. A. holds B. is holding C. doesn't hold

第三部分：**閱讀理解**。共有兩篇短文。閱讀後，每題請根據文章內容選出一個最適合的答案，在答案紙上塗黑作答。

第 26-27 題

Annie, Tina, Tom, and Mike are in the room. There are three cats and a tall tree in Annie's picture. In Tina's picture, there are two pigs near the bikes. How about Tom's picture? There are three tigers and three lions in it. There are some comic books in Mike's picture. They like drawing very much.

📖 room 喜歡　　like 喜歡　　drawing 畫畫

26. What is in Tom's picture?

　　A. Toys.　　　B. Animals.　　　C. Birds.

27. Which is Annie' s picture?

　　A.

　　B.

　　C.

R

The Story of Thanksgiving

In 1620, the Pilgrims went to America from England by ship. They cut down trees to build houses and churches. The Pilgrims had a hard time during the first winter. They didn't have enough food and clothes, so many of them got sick and died. The next spring, the Indians visited them and showed them how to plant corn. They also taught the Pilgrims how to hunt for turkeys in the woods.

When fall came, the Pilgrims had enough food for the winter. They invited the Indians to enjoy a big turkey dinner with them. The Pilgrims were thankful for all the good things and food. That was the first Thanksgiving in the United States. Now, Americans celebrate Thanksgiving on the fourth Thursday of November every year.

📖 Pilgrim 清教徒　　build 建造
die 死亡　　　　Indian 印第安人
hunt 獵捕　　　 woods 森林

28. How did the Pilgrims go to the USA?

A.

B.

C.

29. According to the calendar, what date is Thanksgiving this year?

A. On November nineteenth.

B. On November twentieth.

C. On November twenty-seventh.

November						
SUN	MON	TUE	WED	THU	FRI	SAT
						1
2	3	4	5	6	7	8
9	10	11	12	13	14	15
16	17	18	19	20	21	22
23	24	25	26	27	28	29
30						

30. Which DIDN'T happen before the Indians visited the Pilgrims?

A. The Pilgrims hunted for turkeys in the woods.

B. The Pilgrims had a hard time during the first winter.

C. The Pilgrims cut down trees to build houses and churches.

第四部分：填填看和短句問答。這是出現在家裡備忘欄上的兩張紙條。Niles 寫紙條給他媽媽，訴說他的問題，得到了她的回應和建議。請依照圖片和文章的內容完成這兩封信。注意：答案請寫在答案紙上，第 31-33 題每個空格只需要填一個完整單字。

Question

Dear Mom,

I'm in (例題) **pain** right now. I have a (31) t_____e. It really hurts. I think I need to see a dentist.

Love,

Niles

Answer

Dear Niles,

Go see the dentist right away. She will (32) c_____k your tooth. But in the future, there are a few things you can do to avoid problems with your (33) t_____h:

1. Brush after every meal.
2. Floss regularly.
3. Avoid candy and sweets.

Love,
Mom

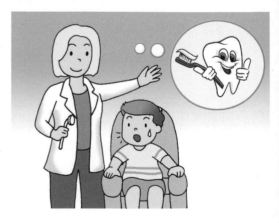

接下來，請根據上面兩封信的內容回答下面的問題。第 34-36 題請用句子回答。

例題：What is bothering Niles? His tooth is bothering him.

34. What is Niles' problem? _____

35. What will Niles do right away? _____

36. What can Niles do to avoid this _____
    problem in the future?

第五部分：重組句子。共四題，請將每題的字詞重組成一個完整且有意義的句子。注意：答案請寫在答案紙上。題目裡的每一個字詞都要用到，增加或減少都會扣分。寫完後記得檢查大小寫和標點符號。首先，請看例題。

例題：There / beautiful / some / flowers. / are

正確答案是： There are some beautiful flowers.

寫完後，請記得檢查大小寫和標點符號。現在我們開始第 37 題。

37. shopping / Many people / department store. / are / the / in

    _____

38. today? / feeling / How / are you

    _____

39. week. / Sandy takes / three times / lessons / a / piano

    _____

40. to you. / talking / when / Listen / to your father / he's

    _____

-☺☺閱讀與寫作結束☺☺-

口說

（一對一面試）

第一部分：暖身、問候	（約 1 分鐘）
老師向學生打招呼	Good morning/afternoon. How are you today? May I have your score sheet? Your number is (准考證號碼).
老師自我介紹	My name is (老師名字). What's your name? How old are you?

第二部分(A)：朗讀句子	（約 1 分鐘）
老師拿出第二部分的圖片和描述圖片的三個句子請考生看	Now, (考生名字), please look at these sentences and this picture. These sentences describe the picture above. They are about a boy's room.
老師確認考生瞭解後，再繼續進行	Do you understand?
老師暫停 10 到 15 秒，讓考生閱讀句子	First, *just look at* the sentences.
老師指示考生開始朗讀句子	Now, *read* the sentences *aloud*.

第二部分(B)：描述圖片	（約 1 分鐘）
老師再一次指向第二部分的圖片	Now, (考生名字), look at the picture again, and answer my questions.
老師指向圖片中的女孩	What is the girl pointing at?
老師指向圖中女孩的洋裝	What color is the girl's dress?
老師指向圖中的時鐘	Where is the clock?

第二部分：朗讀句子、描述圖片

1. The man is seated at the desk.

2. It is noon.

3. There are several items on the floor.

老師給考生看第三部分的四張連環圖	In this part, you are going to tell a story based on these pictures.
老師説明連環圖的主題	These pictures show what happened to Simon and his mother when they were taking a walk at a park last weekend.
老師暫停約 10 秒，讓考生看圖	First, **look at** the four pictures.
待考生準備好，老師再繼續進行	Are you ready?
老師分別指向第 2、3、4 張圖	I will talk about picture 1. Then, you talk about pictures 2, 3, and 4.
老師指向第 1 張圖	Simon and his mother were out looking at butterflies and flowers.
老師分別指向第 2、3、4 張圖，提示考生開始	Now, please talk about pictures 2, 3, and 4.

老師收回第三部分的連環圖	Now, (考生名字), let's talk about you.
老師問考生右列問題	How much time do you spend outdoors?
	What's your favorite color of flower?
	Have you ever caught a butterfly?
測驗結束	Thank you. This is the end of the test. Goodbye.

聽力、閱讀答案紙

Learning

准考證號碼：

SAMPLE

○ 缺考紀錄(考生請勿自行劃記)

聽　力

1 Ⓨ Ⓝ	6 Ⓨ Ⓝ	12 Ⓐ Ⓑ Ⓒ Ⓓ Ⓔ Ⓕ Ⓖ Ⓗ Ⓘ	19 Ⓐ Ⓑ Ⓒ
2 Ⓨ Ⓝ	7 Ⓨ Ⓝ	13 Ⓐ Ⓑ Ⓒ Ⓓ Ⓔ Ⓕ Ⓖ Ⓗ Ⓘ	20 Ⓐ Ⓑ Ⓒ
2 Ⓨ Ⓝ	8 Ⓨ Ⓝ	14 Ⓐ Ⓑ Ⓒ Ⓓ Ⓔ Ⓕ Ⓖ Ⓗ Ⓘ	21 Ⓐ Ⓑ Ⓒ
4 Ⓨ Ⓝ	9 Ⓨ Ⓝ	15 Ⓐ Ⓑ Ⓒ Ⓓ Ⓔ Ⓕ Ⓖ Ⓗ Ⓘ	22 Ⓐ Ⓑ Ⓒ
5 Ⓨ Ⓝ	10 Ⓨ Ⓝ	16 Ⓐ Ⓑ Ⓒ Ⓓ Ⓔ Ⓕ Ⓖ Ⓗ Ⓘ	23 Ⓐ Ⓑ Ⓒ
	11 Ⓨ Ⓝ	17 Ⓐ Ⓑ Ⓒ Ⓓ Ⓔ Ⓕ Ⓖ Ⓗ Ⓘ	24 Ⓐ Ⓑ Ⓒ
		18 Ⓐ Ⓑ Ⓒ Ⓓ Ⓔ Ⓕ Ⓖ Ⓗ Ⓘ	25 Ⓐ Ⓑ Ⓒ

閱　讀

1 Ⓨ Ⓝ	11 Ⓨ Ⓝ	21 Ⓐ Ⓑ Ⓒ
2 Ⓨ Ⓝ	12 Ⓨ Ⓝ	22 Ⓐ Ⓑ Ⓒ
2 Ⓨ Ⓝ	13 Ⓨ Ⓝ	23 Ⓐ Ⓑ Ⓒ
4 Ⓨ Ⓝ	14 Ⓨ Ⓝ	24 Ⓐ Ⓑ Ⓒ
5 Ⓨ Ⓝ	15 Ⓨ Ⓝ	25 Ⓐ Ⓑ Ⓒ
6 Ⓨ Ⓝ	16 Ⓨ Ⓝ	26 Ⓐ Ⓑ Ⓒ
7 Ⓨ Ⓝ	17 Ⓨ Ⓝ	27 Ⓐ Ⓑ Ⓒ
8 Ⓨ Ⓝ	18 Ⓨ Ⓝ	28 Ⓐ Ⓑ Ⓒ
9 Ⓨ Ⓝ	19 Ⓨ Ⓝ	29 Ⓐ Ⓑ Ⓒ
10 Ⓨ Ⓝ	20 Ⓨ Ⓝ	30 Ⓐ Ⓑ Ⓒ

注意事項

1. 限用2B鉛筆作答。
2. 劃記要粗黑、清晰、不可出格，擦拭要清潔。

作答樣例：

正確方式 ●

錯誤方式 ☑ ⊗ ●

學習出版有限公司　　　03797706-30

請沿虛線剪下

Learning

准考證號碼：

例答	pain
31.	
32.	
33.	
例答	His tooth is bothering him.
34.	
35.	
36.	
例答	There are some beautiful flowers.
37.	
38.	
39.	
40.	

跟著百萬網紅「劉毅完美英語」學英文

劉毅老師在「快手」、「抖音」網站，每堂課平均約30秒，每天有2~3堂課，任何時間、任何地點都可以重複練習，在線上從小學、國中、高中、大學到成人，不分年齡、不分程度，人人可學。可和劉毅老師一對一討論，什麼問題都可以問，有問必答！用劉毅老師說的話來留言，寫得愈多，進步愈多，可以輕鬆應付任何考試！

立即掃描QR碼，下載「快手」、「抖音」，搜索「劉毅完美英語」，點讚、分享及關注，成為粉絲，享受免費英語課程！

學習小學英檢試題①題本
Elementary English Proficiency
Model Tests for Kids

售價：220 元

主　　　編 / 李冠勳	
發　行　所 / 學習出版有限公司	☎ (02) 2704-5525
郵 撥 帳 號 / 05127272 學習出版社帳戶	
登　記　證 / 局版台業 2179 號	
印　刷　所 / 文聯彩色印刷有限公司	
台 北 門 市 / 台北市許昌街 17 號 6F	☎ (02) 2331-4060
台灣總經銷 / 紅螞蟻圖書有限公司	☎ (02) 2795-3656
本公司網址 / www.learnbook.com.tw	
電 子 郵 件 / learnbook0928@gmail.com	

2024 年 6 月 1 日新修訂

4713269382355